Breaking Free: A Guide to Conquering Anxiety

Table of Contents:

Chapter 1. Unveiling the Shadow

In the tapestry of human experience, anxiety weaves its threads into the fabric of our lives. It's the knot in the stomach before a big presentation, the racing heartbeat in a crowded room, and the persistent worry that lingers in the quiet moments of the night. Anxiety is an unwelcome companion that many of us grapple with, and in this chapter, we embark on a journey to unveil its shadows and understand its nuances.

Defining Anxiety

Before we can conquer anxiety, we must first unravel its definition. Anxiety is more than just feeling nervous or stressed; it's a complex interplay of thoughts, emotions, and physiological responses. It can manifest in various forms, from generalized anxiety disorder (GAD) to social anxiety, phobias, and panic disorders.

Understanding anxiety involves acknowledging that it's a normal part of the human experience. It's not an enemy to be defeated but a signal from our minds and bodies that something requires our attention. It's the primal fight-or-flight response gone awry in the modern world.

The Impact of Anxiety on Daily Life

Anxiety is not a mere fleeting emotion; it's a force that can significantly impact our daily lives. It can affect our relationships, work, and overall well-being. Imagine a life where simple tasks become monumental challenges and where the fear of the unknown casts a perpetual shadow. In the chapters that follow, we will explore how anxiety influences our thoughts, behaviors, and physical health. We will delve into the ways it can create a distorted lens through which we perceive the world, and how breaking free from its grip requires both self-awareness and strategic interventions.

Embracing the Journey

Embarking on the journey to conquer anxiety is not a declaration of war against oneself but a courageous step toward self-discovery and healing. It's an acknowledgment that, despite the shadows, there is a path toward light. In the chapters ahead, we will unravel practical strategies, personal stories, and the science behind anxiety management.

As we venture into this exploration, remember that you are not alone. Anxiety is a universal experience, and countless individuals have navigated its depths and emerged stronger. This book is your guide, your companion, as we navigate the labyrinth of anxiety and discover the tools to not just survive but thrive.

So, let us begin the journey of breaking free from anxiety's hold, one chapter at a time. The shadows may be long, but they cannot withstand the power of understanding, resilience, and the unwavering human spirit.

Understanding the Landscape of Anxiety

To conquer anxiety, we first embark on a journey of understanding. This section dives into the multifaceted landscape of anxiety, unraveling its diverse manifestations and the ways it can manifest in our thoughts, emotions, and behaviors. By gaining insight into the nuances of anxiety, individuals lay the groundwork for building a resilient mindset and developing effective coping strategies.

Real-life stories and experiences offer glimpses into the diverse ways anxiety can manifest, fostering empathy and a sense of shared understanding among readers. By acknowledging the universal nature of the human experience with anxiety, we create a compassionate space for exploration and growth.

The Interplay of Mind and Body

Anxiety is not confined to the mind alone; its tendrils weave through the very fabric of our bodies. This section explores the intricate interplay between mind and body, delving into the physiological responses that accompany anxious thoughts and emotions. Readers gain insights into the profound impact of stress on the nervous system, sleep patterns, and overall well-being. The chapter emphasizes the mind-body connection as a key element in the quest for conquering anxiety. By recognizing the physical manifestations of anxiety, individuals are empowered to adopt holistic approaches that address both mental and physical aspects of well-being.

Unraveling the Roots of Anxiety

Anxiety often has roots that extend deep into our past experiences, traumas, and belief systems. This section invites readers to explore the origins of their anxiety, fostering a deeper understanding of its underlying causes. Through reflective exercises and self-inquiry, individuals gain insights into the intricate tapestry of factors that contribute to their unique experience of anxiety.

By unraveling the roots of anxiety, readers embark on a journey of self-discovery, acknowledging the complex interplay of nature and nurture in shaping their mental landscape. This chapter sets the stage for the subsequent exploration of strategies to navigate and transform these foundational aspects.

Embracing the Complexity of Emotions

Anxiety is often entwined with a myriad of emotions, from fear and uncertainty to frustration and sadness. This section explores the complexity of emotions, providing tools for individuals to navigate and understand the range of feelings that accompany anxiety. By embracing emotions as messengers that convey valuable information, readers learn to decode the signals their minds and bodies are sending.

The chapter emphasizes that a nuanced understanding of emotions is a crucial element in building emotional intelligence—a key asset in the journey toward conquering anxiety. Through exercises in mindfulness and self-compassion, individuals cultivate a more harmonious relationship with their emotional landscape.

The Decision to Conquer Anxiety

In conclusion, this chapter is a call to action—a decision to confront the shadows of anxiety with courage and curiosity. It lays the foundation for a transformative journey that extends beyond the mere management of symptoms. As we explore the intricate terrain of anxiety, remember that this decision is an affirmation of your resilience and a commitment to a life liberated from the shadows.

The subsequent chapters will build upon these foundations, offering practical strategies, insights, and perspectives to empower individuals on their quest for lasting well-being. In embracing the shadows, we pave the way for the emergence of light, resilience, and the profound joy that comes with conquering anxiety.

Chapter 2. The Anatomy of Anxiety

In our quest to conquer anxiety, it's crucial to dissect its anatomy, peeling back the layers to comprehend its intricacies. Anxiety is not a monolithic entity but a dynamic interplay of thoughts, emotions, and physiological responses. In this chapter, we embark on a voyage to understand the components that make up the tapestry of anxiety.

Different Types of Anxiety Disorders

Anxiety, like a chameleon, takes on various forms, each with its unique characteristics and challenges. From Generalized Anxiety Disorder (GAD), which casts a broad net of worry over everyday life, to Social Anxiety Disorder, where the fear of judgment hinders social interactions, recognizing the specific type of anxiety is the first step towards effective management.
We'll explore the nuances of these disorders, providing insights into their symptoms and how they manifest in real-life situations. Understanding the diversity of anxiety disorders allows us to tailor our strategies, recognizing that what works for one may not work for another.

Unraveling Common Triggers and Causes

Anxiety is not a random assailant; it often has identifiable triggers and root causes. These triggers can range from external stressors such as work pressure, relationship challenges, or financial instability to internal factors like perfectionism and self-criticism. By unraveling the common threads that weave anxiety into our lives, we gain the power to address its sources directly.
We will delve into the role of genetics, brain chemistry, and life experiences in predisposing individuals to anxiety. Understanding the origins of anxiety provides valuable insights into breaking the cycle and developing targeted interventions.

The Vicious Cycle of Anxiety

Anxiety has a way of perpetuating itself, creating a self-reinforcing loop that can feel inescapable. Thoughts fuel emotions, emotions trigger physiological responses, and these responses, in turn, influence our thoughts. Recognizing this cycle is pivotal to interrupting its momentum.
We'll explore how negative thought patterns contribute to anxiety and how breaking these patterns can disrupt the cycle. By understanding the interconnected nature of thoughts, emotions, and physical sensations, we empower ourselves to intervene at various points in the cycle.

A Personal Inventory

Before we can conquer anxiety, we must take stock of our own experiences and patterns. Through reflective exercises and introspection, this chapter encourages readers to create a personal inventory of their anxiety triggers, thought patterns, and physical responses.
As we journey deeper into the anatomy of anxiety, remember that knowledge is power. Armed with an understanding of the various manifestations and triggers, we pave the way for targeted strategies and interventions. The path to conquering anxiety begins with unraveling its intricacies, and in the chapters ahead, we'll explore practical tools to dismantle its grip on our lives.

The Essence of Resilience

Resilience is not a quality reserved for a select few; it is a skill that can be nurtured and developed. This section explores the essence of resilience, framing it as the capacity to bounce back from challenges, adapt to adversity, and emerge stronger from life's trials. Through real-life examples and stories of resilience, readers gain inspiration and insights into the transformative power of this essential quality.
The chapter introduces the concept of a "resilience mindset," emphasizing the role of positive thinking, adaptability, and a sense of empowerment in navigating the complexities of life. By adopting a mindset that views challenges as opportunities for growth, individuals set the stage for a resilient approach to conquering anxiety.

Cultivating Self-Compassion

At the heart of resilience lies self-compassion—an antidote to the self-critical voices that often accompany anxiety. This section guides readers in cultivating a compassionate relationship with themselves. Through mindfulness practices and self-reflection exercises, individuals learn to treat themselves with kindness and understanding, particularly during moments of difficulty.
By acknowledging imperfections and embracing a mindset of self-kindness, individuals lay the foundation for resilience that is anchored in self-love. This chapter reinforces the idea that treating oneself with compassion is not a sign of weakness but a courageous act that fuels the journey toward lasting well-being.

Developing Coping Strategies

Resilience is not a passive quality but an active and dynamic skill that can be honed through intentional practices. This section explores a variety of coping strategies to build resilience in the face of anxiety. From mindfulness and relaxation techniques to problem-solving skills and social support, readers gain a toolkit to navigate challenges with grace and fortitude.
Practical exercises guide individuals in identifying their unique strengths and developing personalized coping strategies that align with their values and goals. The chapter emphasizes that resilience is not about avoiding challenges but about building the capacity to face them with courage and resourcefulness.

Fostering Social Connections

Human connection is a cornerstone of resilience. This section explores the profound impact of social relationships on mental well-being and resilience. Readers gain insights into the reciprocity of support within relationships and the transformative power of shared experiences. By fostering open communication, empathy, and trust, individuals cultivate a network of support that strengthens their resilience.
The chapter also addresses the importance of setting healthy boundaries in relationships—a key aspect of resilient living. By fostering connections that are both supportive and respectful, individuals create a resilient social ecosystem that bolsters their journey toward lasting well-being.

Embracing Flexibility and Adaptability

Resilience is synonymous with adaptability—the ability to bend without breaking in the face of life's storms. This section explores the principles of flexibility and adaptability, offering guidance on how to navigate change with resilience. Readers gain insights into reframing challenges as opportunities for growth and developing a mindset that embraces the uncertainties of life. Through practical exercises and reflection prompts, individuals learn to cultivate a resilient approach to change and uncertainty. The chapter underscores that resilience is not about avoiding challenges or change but about developing the capacity to navigate them with courage and adaptability.

The Journey Ahead

In conclusion, Chapter 2 sets the stage for the journey ahead—an exploration of resilience as the bedrock for conquering anxiety. It is an invitation to cultivate a mindset of empowerment, kindness toward oneself, and the flexibility to navigate life's twists and turns. As we build the foundation of resilience, remember that this journey is a transformative process—a continual unveiling of strength, growth, and the unwavering capacity to conquer anxiety and embrace a life of enduring well-being.

Chapter 3. The Mind-Body Connection: Harmony in Chaos

As we navigate the labyrinth of anxiety, understanding the intricate dance between the mind and body becomes paramount. The mind-body connection is a profound and often underestimated force in shaping our experiences and responses. In this chapter, we unravel the symbiotic relationship between our mental and physical realms, seeking harmony in the chaos of anxiety.

Exploring the Link between Physical and Mental Health

Anxiety is not confined to the mind; it reverberates throughout the body. Racing hearts, tense muscles, and shallow breathing are physical manifestations of the mental turmoil within. By acknowledging this interconnectedness, we gain insights into both the physical toll of anxiety and potential pathways for relief.

We delve into the science behind the mind-body connection, exploring how stress hormones, neurotransmitters, and the autonomic nervous system contribute to the physical symptoms of anxiety. Understanding this link is pivotal in developing holistic strategies that address both mental and physical aspects.

Techniques for Relaxation and Stress Reduction

To disrupt the cycle of anxiety, we must introduce elements of calm and relaxation. This chapter introduces practical techniques that bridge the gap between mind and body, offering tools to alleviate both mental and physical tension.

From deep breathing exercises and progressive muscle relaxation to mindfulness meditation, we explore methods that promote relaxation and counteract the physiological arousal associated with anxiety. These techniques serve as anchors, grounding us in the present moment and providing a sanctuary amid life's storms.

The Power of Movement

Physical activity is not just beneficial for the body; it's a potent elixir for the mind. Exercise has been shown to reduce anxiety by releasing endorphins, the body's natural stress relievers. We discuss how incorporating regular physical activity into our routines can be a game-changer in managing anxiety.

Whether it's a brisk walk, yoga, or a high-energy workout, movement offers a channel for releasing pent-up tension and cultivating a sense of well-being. We explore how finding joy in movement can transform exercise from a chore into a liberating experience.

Integrating Mind-Body Practices into Daily Life

The effectiveness of mind-body practices lies in their integration into daily life. This chapter provides practical tips for seamlessly incorporating relaxation techniques and physical activity into busy schedules. From mindful moments during a hectic workday to finding joy in movement, we explore ways to make these practices sustainable and accessible.

As we navigate the mind-body connection, remember that small changes can yield profound results. By fostering harmony between the mental and physical realms, we pave the way for a more resilient and balanced approach to conquering anxiety. In the chapters ahead, we'll continue to explore practical strategies, building upon the foundation of understanding laid in this exploration of the mind-body connection.

Understanding Mindfulness

At its core, mindfulness is the art of being fully present in the current moment without judgment. This section dissects the essence of mindfulness, emphasizing its role in cultivating awareness of thoughts, emotions, and sensations. Readers embark on a journey to understand the power of the present moment—the sanctuary where anxiety loses its grip and the canvas upon which a mindful life unfolds.

Real-life anecdotes and experiences illustrate the tangible impact of mindfulness on individuals' lives, offering inspiration and insights into the myriad ways it can be integrated into daily living. By grasping the foundational principles of mindfulness, individuals set the stage for a profound shift in their relationship with anxiety.

The Breath as an Anchor

Breath, the rhythmic dance of inhales and exhales, emerges as a central anchor in the practice of mindfulness. This section explores the breath as a grounding force—an ever-present ally that individuals can turn to in moments of heightened anxiety. Through guided exercises and practical techniques, readers learn to use the breath as a focal point, fostering a sense of calm and centeredness.

The chapter encourages individuals to establish a mindful breathing practice—a simple yet powerful tool that can be accessed anytime, anywhere. By anchoring themselves in the breath, individuals create a sanctuary within, offering respite from the storms of anxious thoughts.

Cultivating Mindful Awareness

Mindfulness extends beyond formal practices; it is a way of seeing and engaging with the world. This section delves into the cultivation of mindful awareness in daily life. From savoring the sensory richness of experiences to embracing non-judgmental observation of thoughts and emotions, readers gain practical insights into infusing mindfulness into routine activities.

By developing mindful awareness, individuals learn to step back from automatic reactions and cultivate a spacious presence in each moment. This chapter serves as a guide for incorporating mindfulness into everyday life, turning mundane moments into opportunities for profound connection and serenity.

Mindfulness Meditation: A Journey Inward

Meditation becomes a vessel for the inward journey—an exploration of the landscapes of the mind and the cultivation of inner stillness. This section introduces mindfulness meditation, offering step-by-step guidance for individuals to embark on their own contemplative journey. Through practices such as body scan, loving-kindness meditation, and focused attention, readers discover the diverse ways in which meditation can become a source of tranquility and insight.

The chapter emphasizes that mindfulness meditation is not about silencing the mind but about observing it with gentle curiosity. By establishing a regular meditation practice, individuals embark on a transformative journey that extends beyond the meditation cushion and permeates every facet of their lives.

Mindfulness-Based Stress Reduction (MBSR)

Structured mindfulness programs, such as Mindfulness-Based Stress Reduction (MBSR), emerge as comprehensive frameworks for conquering anxiety. This section explores the principles of MBSR, offering insights into its origins, core practices, and the empirical evidence supporting its effectiveness in reducing anxiety and enhancing well-being.

The chapter encourages individuals to explore mindfulness programs, either through structured courses or self-guided practices, as a holistic approach to conquering anxiety. By immersing themselves in the principles of MBSR, individuals embark on a transformative journey that integrates mindfulness into the very fabric of their existence.

The Embodied Practice of Mindful Movement

Mindfulness extends beyond stillness; it finds expression in the graceful movements of the body. This section explores mindful movement practices, such as yoga and tai chi, as avenues for conquering anxiety. Readers gain insights into how intentional, mindful movement can become a form of meditation in motion—a way to cultivate physical well-being and mental clarity. Practical tips for incorporating mindful movement into daily routines are provided, encouraging individuals to explore the synergies between breath, body, and mind. By embracing mindful movement, individuals expand their repertoire of tools for conquering anxiety and fostering holistic well-being.

The Integration of Mindfulness into Daily Living

In conclusion, Chapter 3 underscores the integration of mindfulness into the very fabric of daily living. It is an invitation to approach each moment with a spirit of presence and a heart open to the richness of experience. As individuals delve into mindfulness practices, remember that the journey is not about perfection but about the continual exploration and cultivation of awareness. The subsequent chapters will continue to unfold as we weave mindfulness into the narrative of conquering anxiety. By embracing the transformative power of mindfulness, individuals not only illuminate the shadows of anxiety but also embark on a journey toward enduring peace, resilience, and the profound joy of living fully in the present moment.

Chapter 4. Identifying and Challenging Negative Thoughts

In the intricate tapestry of anxiety, negative thoughts are the threads that often weave the most complex patterns. This chapter is a journey into the realm of cognitive processes, where we uncover the power of thoughts in shaping our emotional landscape. By identifying and challenging these negative thoughts, we unravel a crucial layer in the fabric of anxiety.

Cognitive Behavioral Therapy (CBT) Principles

Cognitive Behavioral Therapy, or CBT, stands as a beacon in the realm of anxiety management. At its core, CBT recognizes the profound connection between thoughts, emotions, and behaviors. This chapter introduces the fundamental principles of CBT, emphasizing its role in breaking the cycle of anxiety by transforming negative thought patterns.
We explore how thoughts, feelings, and behaviors are interconnected, creating a dynamic system that can either perpetuate or alleviate anxiety. Through practical examples and case studies, readers gain insights into the ways CBT can be applied to their own lives.

Practical Exercises to Restructure Negative Thinking

Armed with the principles of CBT, we embark on practical exercises designed to restructure negative thinking. From identifying automatic thoughts to challenging cognitive distortions, these exercises provide tangible tools for dismantling the thought patterns that fuel anxiety.
Through journaling, self-reflection, and guided exercises, readers learn to recognize the patterns of negative thinking unique to their experience. This chapter serves as a workshop, empowering individuals to become active participants in reshaping their mental landscape.

The Power of Affirmations and Positive Self-Talk

In the battlefield of anxiety, affirmations and positive self-talk stand as powerful allies. This section explores the science behind the impact of language on our thoughts and emotions. By cultivating a positive internal dialogue, we can gradually shift the narrative from self-doubt to self-empowerment.
We provide practical tips for creating personalized affirmations and incorporating positive self-talk into daily routines. These tools act as a counterforce to the persistent negativity that often accompanies anxiety, fostering a mindset of resilience and optimism.

Navigating Setbacks and Building Resilience

The journey to conquer anxiety is not linear, and setbacks are an inevitable part of the process. This chapter addresses the challenges that may arise during the practice of identifying and challenging negative thoughts. By understanding the nature of setbacks and cultivating resilience, individuals are better equipped to navigate the twists and turns on the path to mental well-being.

As we delve into the realm of thoughts and their impact on anxiety, remember that this journey is not about eradicating all negative thoughts but developing the skills to navigate them effectively. In the chapters ahead, we will continue to build upon this foundation, exploring additional strategies and perspectives that contribute to a resilient and empowered mindset.

The Power of Thoughts

Our thoughts weave the narrative of our experiences, and in the realm of anxiety, they often take on a script of worry, self-doubt, and fear. This section delves into the power of thoughts, exploring how they shape emotions and behaviors. Readers gain insights into the intricate dance between thoughts and anxiety, setting the stage for the empowering journey of cognitive restructuring.

By understanding the cognitive landscape, individuals become adept at identifying automatic negative thoughts—the whispers of anxiety that influence their perception of reality. This foundational awareness becomes the catalyst for the transformative process of cognitive restructuring.

Cognitive Restructuring: Unveiling the Process

Cognitive restructuring is akin to reshaping the architecture of the mind. This section unveils the process, guiding readers through the steps of identifying, challenging, and reframing distorted thoughts. Real-life examples illustrate the practical application of cognitive restructuring, offering a roadmap for individuals to navigate the labyrinth of anxious thinking.

The chapter introduces cognitive distortions—the common patterns of biased thinking that contribute to anxiety. Through exercises and self-reflection, individuals learn to recognize and challenge these distortions, opening the door to a more balanced and rational perspective.

The Role of Self-Talk

The inner dialogue we have with ourselves—the self-talk—holds immense power in shaping our emotional landscape. This section explores the role of self-talk in anxiety and introduces the concept of positive affirmations. Readers gain insights into how intentional, positive self-talk can become a powerful tool in the process of cognitive restructuring.

Practical exercises guide individuals in crafting their own affirmations, fostering a mindset that is supportive, optimistic, and aligned with their goals. By harnessing the power of positive self-talk, individuals lay the foundation for a more resilient and empowered mindset.

Challenging Core Beliefs

Deep-seated beliefs about oneself, the world, and the future often underlie anxious thinking. This section invites readers to explore and challenge core beliefs that contribute to anxiety.

Through reflective exercises and guided questioning, individuals gain insights into the origins of these beliefs and their impact on their mental well-being.

The chapter emphasizes the importance of fostering a growth mindset—an outlook that views challenges as opportunities for learning and development. By challenging and reframing core beliefs, individuals cultivate a mindset that is adaptive, resilient, and conducive to conquering anxiety.

Creating a Cognitive Restructuring Toolbox

Cognitive restructuring is not a one-size-fits-all process; it is a personalized journey of self-discovery. This section guides individuals in creating their own cognitive restructuring toolbox—a collection of techniques and strategies that resonate with their unique needs and preferences. From journaling and thought records to visualization and mindfulness, readers gain insights into the diverse tools that can be integrated into their cognitive restructuring practice. The chapter encourages individuals to experiment with different techniques, fostering a sense of agency and creativity in the process. By creating a cognitive restructuring toolbox, individuals empower themselves to navigate the landscape of thoughts with skill and resilience.

The Continued Journey

In conclusion, Chapter 4 marks a significant point in the journey of conquering anxiety. It is an exploration into the art of reframing thoughts, challenging negative beliefs, and cultivating a mindset that empowers rather than constrains. As individuals delve into the process of cognitive restructuring, remember that it is a dynamic and ongoing journey—a continual process of refining and reshaping the narrative of one's life.

The subsequent chapters will build upon these foundations, offering additional strategies and perspectives to further empower individuals on their quest for enduring well-being. By mastering the art of cognitive restructuring, individuals not only shift the sands of anxious thinking but also lay the groundwork for a more resilient, positive, and empowered approach to life's challenges.

Chapter 5. Building a Support System

In the labyrinth of anxiety, the journey becomes more bearable when accompanied by a supportive network. This chapter delves into the importance of forging connections and building a robust support system. From family and friends to professional allies, cultivating a network of understanding individuals is a key component in the quest to conquer anxiety.

The Importance of Social Connections

Humans are inherently social beings, and our connections with others play a profound role in our mental well-being. This section explores the impact of social support on anxiety, emphasizing the healing power of empathetic relationships. We delve into the science behind social connections, examining how positive interactions can buffer against the challenges posed by anxiety.

Communicating with Friends and Family about Anxiety

Opening up about anxiety can be a transformative yet daunting step. This chapter provides practical guidance on communicating with friends and family about anxiety, offering insights into fostering understanding and empathy. It explores the art of expressing one's needs and boundaries while also equipping loved ones with the tools to offer meaningful support. Through anecdotes and real-life examples, readers gain perspectives on the diverse ways individuals have navigated these conversations. By bridging the gap between silence and understanding, we pave the way for stronger, more compassionate connections.

Seeking Professional Support

While friends and family provide invaluable support, professional help can be a crucial pillar in anxiety management. This section outlines the various mental health professionals available, from therapists and counselors to psychiatrists. It offers guidance on how to initiate the search for the right professional and provides insights into the different therapeutic approaches. Understanding that seeking professional support is a courageous step toward healing, this chapter aims to destigmatize the process. It emphasizes that reaching out for help is not a sign of weakness but a testament to resilience and a commitment to personal growth.

Group Support and Community Resources

In addition to individual connections, group support can be a powerful tool in the battle against anxiety. This section explores the benefits of group therapy and community resources. Whether in-person or online, shared experiences with others who understand the challenges of anxiety can foster a sense of belonging and reduce feelings of isolation.

15

From local support groups to online forums, we navigate the landscape of community resources, offering readers a roadmap to discover environments where they can share, learn, and grow alongside others on similar journeys.

Nurturing Relationships for Long-Term Well-Being

Building a support system is not a one-time effort but an ongoing process that requires nurturing and cultivation. This chapter concludes with insights into maintaining healthy relationships for long-term well-being. It explores the reciprocity of support, emphasizing that being part of a community involves both giving and receiving.

As we journey through the dynamics of support systems, remember that in forging connections, we create a web of strength that helps navigate the complexities of anxiety. The chapters ahead will continue to unravel practical strategies, reinforcing the foundation of understanding and resilience built thus far.

The Emotional Landscape

Emotions, like waves, rise and fall within the vast landscape of our inner world. This section delves into the complexity of emotions, exploring their diverse nature and the pivotal role they play in our daily lives. Readers gain insights into the profound impact of emotions on mental well-being and how they intersect with the fabric of anxiety.

The chapter invites individuals to embrace a non-judgmental awareness of their emotions—a foundational practice in the cultivation of emotional resilience. By understanding the nuances of their emotional landscape, individuals embark on a journey to regulate and navigate their feelings with skill and grace.

The Art of Emotional Resilience

Emotional resilience is the capacity to bounce back from challenges, adapt to adversity, and thrive in the face of life's emotional storms. This section explores the art of emotional resilience, offering practical insights and strategies for building this essential quality. Real-life examples illustrate the transformative power of emotional resilience in conquering anxiety.

The chapter introduces the concept of emotional regulation—the ability to modulate and manage one's emotions effectively. Through exercises in mindfulness, self-awareness, and cognitive restructuring, individuals develop a repertoire of skills to navigate the tumultuous currents of emotions with resilience and self-compassion.

Mindfulness and Emotional Regulation

Mindfulness, a steadfast companion on our journey, emerges once again as a guiding light in the realm of emotional regulation. This section explores how mindfulness practices can be harnessed to cultivate emotional resilience. Readers gain practical tools for observing and accepting their emotions without being overwhelmed by them.

Guided mindfulness exercises for emotional awareness and regulation are provided, encouraging individuals to anchor themselves in the present moment and create a space for intentional responses to their emotions. By infusing mindfulness into their emotional landscape, individuals foster a resilient and balanced relationship with their feelings.

Cognitive Strategies for Emotional Regulation

Cognitive strategies, familiar companions from the journey of cognitive restructuring, make a return in the context of emotional regulation. This section guides individuals in applying cognitive techniques to navigate and regulate their emotional responses. From reframing thoughts to challenging emotional biases, readers gain insights into the interconnectedness of cognitive and emotional well-being.

Practical exercises and thought experiments empower individuals to reshape their emotional responses through intentional cognitive processes. By integrating cognitive strategies into their emotional toolkit, individuals amplify their capacity for emotional resilience and regulation.

Expressive and Creative Approaches

Emotions find expression in myriad forms, and creative outlets become powerful tools for emotional regulation. This section explores the transformative potential of expressive and creative approaches, such as art, writing, and movement. Readers discover how these outlets provide a cathartic release for emotions and serve as vehicles for self-discovery and healing. The chapter encourages individuals to explore different creative modalities, fostering a sense of agency and empowerment in their emotional journey. By engaging in expressive practices, individuals not only regulate their emotions but also tap into a wellspring of resilience and self-expression.

Building Supportive Relationships

The strength of social connections reverberates in the landscape of emotional resilience. This section explores the role of relationships in fostering emotional well-being and regulation. Real-life stories highlight the transformative impact of supportive connections on individuals' ability to navigate and regulate their emotions.

The chapter emphasizes the reciprocity of emotional support within relationships, encouraging individuals to communicate openly, seek understanding, and provide support to others. By building and maintaining supportive relationships, individuals create a resilient social network that enhances their emotional well-being.

Cultivating a Positive Emotional Climate

In conclusion, Chapter 5 unfolds as a guide to cultivating a positive emotional climate—an environment that nourishes emotional resilience and regulation. It is an exploration into the art of understanding, navigating, and transforming emotions in the pursuit of enduring well-being. As individuals delve into the practices and strategies outlined in this chapter, remember that the journey of emotional resilience is a continual process—an evolving dance with the rich tapestry of feelings.

The subsequent chapters will continue to unveil additional insights and tools, building upon the foundations of emotional resilience and regulation. By mastering the art of understanding and navigating emotions, individuals not only conquer anxiety but also foster a life characterized by emotional balance, authenticity, and enduring well-being.

Chapter 6. Mindfulness and Meditation: Finding Calm Amidst the Chaos

In the hustle and bustle of modern life, the art of mindfulness and meditation emerges as a sanctuary for the anxious mind. This chapter is a voyage into the realm of present-moment awareness, offering tools to navigate the turbulent waters of anxiety with a calm and centered spirit.

Techniques for Grounding and Staying Present

Mindfulness is the practice of being fully present in the current moment, and this section explores techniques for grounding oneself amid the swirl of anxious thoughts. From focused breathing exercises to sensory awareness, readers will discover practical methods to anchor their attention to the present and break free from the grip of anxiety.

We delve into the concept of mindful awareness, examining how it can be cultivated in everyday activities. By incorporating mindfulness into routine tasks, readers learn to infuse moments of stillness into their busy lives.

The Transformative Power of Meditation

Meditation, a cousin to mindfulness, offers a deeper exploration into the recesses of the mind. This chapter introduces various meditation practices, from guided imagery and loving-kindness meditation to body scan and transcendental meditation. Each method is a unique tool in the arsenal against anxiety, providing a path to inner stillness and clarity.

Through guided exercises and reflections, readers are encouraged to explore different meditation styles, finding the one that resonates most with their preferences and needs. The transformative power of meditation lies in its ability to cultivate a sense of inner peace that transcends the chaos of external circumstances.

Integrating Mindfulness into Daily Life

The true essence of mindfulness is not confined to designated meditation sessions but extends into the fabric of daily life. This section provides practical insights into integrating mindfulness into everyday activities, transforming mundane moments into opportunities for presence and self-awareness.

From mindful eating to walking meditation, readers discover how to infuse intention and attention into their daily routines. The goal is to create a sustainable and realistic approach to mindfulness, making it a seamless part of life rather than an isolated practice.

Embracing the Silence Within

In a world filled with noise and distraction, embracing the silence within becomes a radical act of self-care. This chapter explores the benefits of cultivating moments of stillness and quiet reflection. Whether through solitude, nature walks, or technology detoxes, readers learn to carve out spaces for silence in their lives, fostering a deeper connection with themselves.

The Journey of Self-Discovery

Mindfulness and meditation are not merely tools for anxiety management; they are gateways to self-discovery. This chapter concludes by highlighting the transformative journey that individuals embark upon as they deepen their mindfulness practice. By cultivating a mindful and meditative approach to life, readers uncover insights into their own thought patterns, emotional responses, and the interconnected nature of mind and body.

As we navigate the realm of mindfulness and meditation, remember that these practices are not quick fixes but lifelong companions on the journey to conquer anxiety. The subsequent chapters will build upon these foundations, exploring additional strategies and perspectives to further empower individuals in their quest for mental well-being.

The Mind-Body Connection

The intricate dance between mind and body is a central theme in this exploration of lasting well-being. This section delves into the profound connection between lifestyle choices and mental health, unraveling how factors such as nutrition, physical activity, sleep, and stress management contribute to the holistic tapestry of well-being.

Readers gain insights into the bidirectional relationship between the mind and body, understanding that choices made in one domain can reverberate in the other. This foundational awareness becomes the catalyst for the transformative journey of nurturing healthy lifestyle habits.

Nutrition as Nourishment for the Mind

The food we consume serves not only as fuel for the body but also as nourishment for the mind. This section explores the impact of nutrition on mental health, highlighting the role of a balanced and nutrient-rich diet in promoting cognitive function, mood regulation, and overall well-being. Practical tips for incorporating brain-boosting foods, such as omega-3 fatty acids, antioxidants, and whole grains, are provided. The chapter also addresses the relationship between gut health and mental well-being, emphasizing the importance of a healthy digestive system in supporting emotional resilience.

The Joy of Movement

Physical activity becomes a joyful expression of well-being in this section, as individuals discover the transformative power of exercise in conquering anxiety. Readers explore the diverse ways in which movement—whether through structured workouts, outdoor activities, or mindful practices—can positively impact mental health.

The chapter introduces the concept of "exercise as medicine," highlighting the role of physical activity in reducing stress, improving mood, and enhancing cognitive function. Practical suggestions for incorporating movement into daily life empower individuals to find joy and fulfillment in staying active.

The Rhythms of Sleep

Amidst the hustle and bustle of modern life, the significance of quality sleep often takes center stage in the quest for well-being. This section unfolds as a guide to understanding the rhythms of sleep and their profound impact on mental health. Readers gain insights into the importance of establishing healthy sleep hygiene practices and cultivating a restful nighttime routine.
The chapter addresses common sleep challenges, such as insomnia and irregular sleep patterns, offering practical strategies to promote better sleep. By embracing the rhythms of rest, individuals set the stage for improved mood, cognitive function, and overall resilience in the face of anxiety.

Stress Management and Mindfulness

In the whirlwind of daily life, stress emerges as a ubiquitous companion, influencing mental well-being and anxiety levels. This section explores the art of stress management, guiding individuals to develop strategies that mitigate the impact of stress on their mental health. Mindfulness, a familiar ally in the journey, takes center stage once again as a powerful tool for stress reduction. Readers discover how mindfulness practices, such as meditation, deep breathing, and progressive muscle relaxation, can become anchors in navigating the challenges of stress.

Cultivating Healthy Relationships

The quality of relationships becomes a cornerstone of lasting well-being in this section. Readers explore the transformative impact of positive social connections on mental health, emphasizing the reciprocity of support within relationships.
The chapter provides insights into effective communication, boundary-setting, and the cultivation of healthy relationships. By fostering connections that are supportive, authentic, and nurturing, individuals create a social ecosystem that fortifies their mental well-being.

Balancing Work and Life

In the modern landscape, the demands of work often intersect with the quest for well-being. This section explores the art of balancing work and life, offering practical strategies to create a harmonious and fulfilling existence.
Readers gain insights into time management, setting boundaries, and cultivating a sense of purpose in both professional and personal domains. By embracing a balanced approach to life, individuals enhance their resilience and create a foundation for enduring well-being.

The Holistic Picture of Well-Being

In conclusion, Chapter 6 unveils the holistic picture of well-being—a canvas painted with the brushstrokes of nutritious choices, joyful movement, restful sleep, stress management, meaningful connections, and a balanced life. It is an invitation to consider the profound impact of lifestyle habits on mental health and to embark on a transformative journey of nurturing well-being from the inside out.

The subsequent chapters will continue to unveil additional dimensions of lasting well-being, offering insights and tools to further empower individuals on their quest to conquer anxiety. By integrating healthy lifestyle habits into the fabric of their lives, individuals not only create a resilient foundation for well-being but also embark on a journey of enduring joy, fulfillment, and mental flourishing.

Chapter 7. Healthy Lifestyle Habits: Nourishing Body and Mind

In the symphony of anxiety management, the role of a healthy lifestyle serves as a foundational note, influencing both body and mind. This chapter delves into the transformative impact of nutrition, exercise, and sleep on mental well-being, offering a holistic approach to breaking free from the chains of anxiety.

The Role of Nutrition in Mental Health

The food we consume is more than mere sustenance; it is a potent influencer of our mental health. This section explores the connection between nutrition and anxiety, examining the impact of dietary choices on mood and cognitive function. Readers gain insights into the role of essential nutrients, gut health, and hydration in fostering a balanced mental state.
Practical tips and dietary recommendations are provided, empowering individuals to make informed choices that support their mental well-being. From mood-boosting foods to the importance of a well-balanced diet, this chapter aims to guide readers toward nourishing their bodies and minds.

Exercise as a Stress-Busting Ally

Physical activity is a formidable ally in the battle against anxiety. This section explores the science behind exercise and its ability to reduce stress hormones, release endorphins, and improve overall mood. Whether it's a brisk walk, a yoga session, or a high-intensity workout, readers discover the diverse ways in which movement contributes to mental well-being.
The chapter also addresses the common barriers to exercise and provides practical strategies for incorporating physical activity into diverse lifestyles. By reframing exercise as a joyful and empowering endeavor, individuals can transform it from a chore into a source of resilience.

Creating a Balanced Routine

Consistency and routine offer a sense of stability in the face of life's uncertainties. This section emphasizes the importance of establishing a balanced daily routine that incorporates healthy habits. From sleep hygiene to time management, readers gain insights into creating a rhythm that nurtures both body and mind.
Practical suggestions for integrating self-care practices, work responsibilities, and leisure activities are provided, helping individuals strike a harmonious balance that promotes mental well-being. The goal is to cultivate a routine that fosters resilience and provides a reliable framework for navigating the challenges of daily life.

Adequate Sleep: The Pillar of Mental Health

Quality sleep is a cornerstone of mental health, and this section explores the profound impact of sleep on anxiety. Readers gain an understanding of the sleep-anxiety relationship, learning practical strategies for improving sleep hygiene and cultivating restful nights.

From creating a tranquil sleep environment to establishing bedtime rituals, this chapter guides individuals in fostering healthy sleep patterns. Recognizing the significance of restorative sleep as a pillar of mental well-being, readers are empowered to make intentional choices that support their journey to conquer anxiety.

The Interconnected Dance of Body and Mind

In conclusion, this chapter underscores the interconnected dance of body and mind in the tapestry of anxiety management. By embracing a holistic approach that nourishes both physical and mental well-being, individuals lay a robust foundation for lasting transformation. As we navigate the realms of nutrition, exercise, and sleep, remember that each choice is a step toward empowerment and resilience in the pursuit of a life liberated from anxiety. The subsequent chapters will continue to build upon this foundation, exploring additional strategies and perspectives to further empower individuals on their quest for mental well-being.

Embracing the Present Moment

The essence of mindful living lies in the ability to fully embrace the present moment. This section delves into the transformative power of mindfulness, guiding individuals to cultivate a heightened awareness of their thoughts, emotions, and surroundings. Readers gain insights into the practice of being fully engaged in the here and now—a sanctuary where anxiety dissipates, and a profound sense of peace unfolds.

Real-life examples illustrate the impact of mindfulness on mental well-being, highlighting its role in reducing rumination, enhancing focus, and fostering a sense of calm. The chapter introduces simple mindfulness exercises that individuals can integrate into their daily lives, empowering them to savor the richness of each moment.

Finding Purpose and Meaning

Purpose becomes a guiding star in the journey toward lasting well-being. This section invites individuals to explore the concept of purpose and its profound impact on mental health. Readers gain insights into the transformative potential of aligning their actions with core values, cultivating a sense of meaning, and contributing to something greater than themselves.

Practical exercises guide individuals in uncovering their personal values, clarifying their aspirations, and infusing purpose into their daily lives. By aligning their actions with a sense of purpose, individuals not only create a roadmap for enduring well-being but also discover a source of resilience and joy.

Gratitude and Joy in Everyday Moments

Gratitude emerges as a beacon of positivity in the landscape of mindful living. This section explores the practice of cultivating gratitude, guiding individuals to appreciate and acknowledge the blessings in their lives. Readers discover how the intentional cultivation of gratitude can shift their focus from anxiety-inducing thoughts to the abundance of positive experiences.

The chapter introduces gratitude journaling, mindfulness-based gratitude practices, and the art of savoring as tools to enhance the experience of joy in everyday moments. By fostering a mindset of gratitude, individuals create a foundation for enduring well-being and a heightened awareness of the beauty that surrounds them.

Mindful Communication and Connection

In the realm of relationships, mindful communication becomes a cornerstone of lasting well-being. This section unfolds as a guide to cultivating presence, empathy, and authenticity in interpersonal connections. Real-life stories illuminate the transformative impact of mindful communication on the quality of relationships.

Practical tips for active listening, empathetic communication, and the cultivation of mindfulness in relationships empower individuals to navigate the complexities of connection with grace and intention. By fostering mindful communication, individuals create a social landscape that nurtures their mental well-being and contributes to a sense of belonging.

Mindfulness in Daily Activities

Mindful living extends beyond formal practices; it is a way of approaching everyday activities with presence and intention. This section explores how individuals can infuse mindfulness into routine tasks, transforming them into opportunities for connection and joy. Readers gain insights into mindful eating, mindful walking, and the art of bringing awareness to daily rituals.

Practical exercises guide individuals in incorporating mindfulness into their daily routines, fostering a sense of tranquility and purpose in even the most mundane activities. By embracing mindfulness in daily life, individuals create a tapestry of well-being woven with intention, attention, and a profound appreciation for the richness of each moment.

Cultivating Resilience through Mindful Living

In conclusion, Chapter 7 unfolds as an exploration into the art of mindful living—a practice that transcends the boundaries of anxiety and ushers individuals into a life characterized by presence, purpose, and joy. It is an invitation to savor the beauty of each moment, infuse meaning into daily life, and foster connections that nurture the soul.

The subsequent chapters will continue to unveil additional dimensions of mindful living, offering insights and practices to further empower individuals on their quest to conquer anxiety. By embracing the art of mindful living, individuals not only illuminate the shadows of anxiety but also embark on a journey toward enduring well-being, resilience, and a deep appreciation for the precious gift of the present moment.

Chapter 8. Professional Help and Resources: Guiding the Way

In the tapestry of conquering anxiety, seeking professional help is a pivotal thread that adds strength and resilience to the weave. This chapter explores the array of mental health professionals, therapeutic approaches, and available resources, guiding individuals on their journey towards sustainable well-being.

Therapy Options: Counseling, Psychotherapy, Medication

Understanding the diverse landscape of therapeutic interventions is crucial in creating a personalized approach to anxiety management. This section provides an overview of counseling, psychotherapy, and medication as viable options. Readers gain insights into the distinctions between these modalities, empowering them to make informed decisions about their mental health care.

The chapter also explores the concept of a therapeutic alliance, emphasizing the importance of a strong and trusting relationship between individuals and their mental health professionals. By demystifying the therapeutic process, readers are encouraged to approach therapy as a collaborative and transformative endeavor.

Finding the Right Mental Health Professional

Choosing the right mental health professional is a significant step in the journey to conquer anxiety. This section offers practical guidance on the process of finding a therapist or counselor who aligns with individual needs and goals. From researching specialties to conducting initial consultations, readers gain insights into the criteria for selecting a mental health professional best suited for their journey.

Real-life stories and testimonials illustrate the diverse paths individuals have taken to find the right mental health support. By acknowledging that the process is unique for each person, this chapter aims to alleviate apprehensions and facilitate a smoother entry into the therapeutic journey.

Teletherapy and Online Resources

The landscape of mental health support has expanded with the advent of teletherapy and online resources. This section explores the benefits and considerations of virtual therapy, providing insights into the accessibility and convenience it offers. Readers discover the wealth of online resources, from mental health apps to educational websites, that complement their journey towards mental well-being.

In a world where geographical barriers are diminishing, individuals are encouraged to explore the array of options available at their fingertips. The chapter highlights the importance of leveraging technology as a tool for enhancing mental health support.

The Stigma Surrounding Mental Health

Despite progress in mental health awareness, stigma remains a formidable barrier. This section addresses the societal perceptions surrounding mental health, offering perspectives on how individuals can navigate and challenge stigma. By fostering open conversations and promoting mental health literacy, readers are empowered to contribute to a more supportive and understanding community.

Navigating Insurance and Financial Considerations

The practical aspects of seeking professional help, such as insurance coverage and financial considerations, are often significant considerations. This chapter provides practical advice on navigating insurance policies, understanding coverage for mental health services, and exploring alternative resources for financial assistance. By demystifying the financial aspect of mental health care, individuals can approach the process with clarity and confidence.

The Continual Journey of Self-Discovery

In conclusion, this chapter emphasizes that seeking professional help is not a one-time event but a continual journey of self-discovery and growth. Mental health care is a dynamic and evolving process that adapts to the changing needs of individuals. As we explore the avenues of therapy and professional support, remember that each step is a courageous stride toward a life liberated from the shadows of anxiety. The subsequent chapters will build upon these foundations, exploring additional strategies and perspectives to further empower individuals on their quest for mental well-being.

Understanding Resilient Thinking

Resilient thinking is a dynamic mindset that reframes challenges as opportunities for growth, views setbacks as temporary, and embraces a positive perspective on life. This section delves into the core principles of resilient thinking, guiding individuals to cultivate a mindset that not only mitigates anxiety but also fosters enduring well-being.
Readers gain insights into the psychological underpinnings of resilient thinking, understanding how cognitive patterns influence emotional responses and behavior. Real-life stories illuminate the transformative impact of resilient thinking on individuals' ability to navigate life's twists and turns with resilience and optimism.

Reframing Challenges as Opportunities

At the heart of resilient thinking lies the ability to reframe challenges as opportunities for learning and growth. This section unfolds as a guide to embracing a mindset that sees adversity as a stepping stone rather than an insurmountable obstacle.

Practical exercises and thought experiments empower individuals to reframe their perspectives on challenges, fostering a sense of empowerment and resilience. By viewing difficulties through the lens of opportunity, individuals not only conquer anxiety in the moment but also cultivate a mindset that propels them toward lasting well-being.

Cultivating a Positive Outlook

Positivity becomes a beacon in the journey toward resilient thinking. This section explores the art of cultivating a positive outlook on life, guiding individuals to focus on strengths, celebrate successes, and savor moments of joy. Readers discover how intentional shifts in perspective can profoundly influence their emotional well-being.

The chapter introduces positivity practices, such as gratitude, positive affirmations, and visualization, as tools to cultivate a more optimistic mindset. By nurturing a positive outlook, individuals create a reservoir of resilience that sustains them through the challenges of life.

Building Self-Efficacy and Confidence

Resilient thinking is intertwined with a sense of self-efficacy—the belief in one's ability to influence outcomes through effort and perseverance. This section explores the connection between resilient thinking and the development of self-efficacy, guiding individuals to build confidence in their capacity to navigate challenges.

Practical strategies for setting and achieving realistic goals, learning from experiences, and building a repertoire of coping skills empower individuals to enhance their self-efficacy. By cultivating confidence in their abilities, individuals not only conquer anxiety in the moment but also lay the groundwork for enduring resilience.

Flexibility in Thinking

Resilient thinking embraces flexibility—a willingness to adapt and adjust in the face of changing circumstances. This section explores the role of flexible thinking in resilience, guiding individuals to challenge rigid thought patterns and embrace a more adaptive mindset.

Real-life examples illustrate the transformative impact of flexible thinking on individuals' ability to navigate uncertainty and ambiguity. The chapter provides practical exercises to enhance cognitive flexibility, empowering individuals to approach challenges with openness and creativity.

Learning from Setbacks

Resilient thinking acknowledges that setbacks are a natural part of life's journey. This section unfolds as a guide to learning from setbacks, guiding individuals to extract lessons, cultivate resilience, and pivot toward growth. Readers gain insights into the importance of self-compassion in the face of setbacks and the role of reflection in the learning process.

Practical exercises empower individuals to reframe setbacks as opportunities for self-discovery and refinement. By approaching setbacks with a resilient mindset, individuals not only conquer anxiety in the aftermath of challenges but also emerge stronger and more resilient.

Navigating Uncertainty with Resilience

In conclusion, Chapter 8 unveils the power of resilient thinking—a mindset that propels individuals beyond the constraints of anxiety and into a life characterized by adaptability, optimism, and enduring well-being. It is an exploration into the art of thriving in adversity, reframing challenges, and navigating uncertainty with resilience.

The subsequent chapters will continue to unveil additional dimensions of resilient thinking, offering insights and practices to further empower individuals on their quest to conquer anxiety. By embracing resilient thinking, individuals not only illuminate the shadows of anxiety but also forge a path toward lasting well-being, thriving in the face of life's challenges with a mindset that is resilient, optimistic, and profoundly transformative.

Chapter 9. Overcoming Fear and Avoidance: The Path to Liberation

In the intricate dance of anxiety, fear and avoidance often take center stage, casting a shadow on the path to healing. This chapter is a courageous exploration into facing fears, confronting avoidance behaviors, and embracing the transformative power of stepping outside comfort zones.

Gradual Exposure and Desensitization

Fear, though formidable, loses its grip in the face of intentional and gradual exposure. This section introduces the concept of systematic desensitization, a therapeutic approach that involves facing fears in a structured and incremental manner. Readers gain insights into how breaking down anxiety-provoking situations into manageable steps can foster a sense of control and mastery.

Real-life examples and case studies illustrate the transformative journey of individuals who have embraced gradual exposure. By highlighting the resilience and courage of those who confronted their fears, this chapter aims to inspire and guide readers on their own path to liberation.

Setting Realistic Goals for Progress

In the pursuit of overcoming anxiety, setting realistic and achievable goals becomes a compass guiding the way. This section explores the art of goal-setting, emphasizing the importance of clarity, specificity, and flexibility. Readers learn to identify small, tangible steps that align with their aspirations, fostering a sense of accomplishment and motivation.

Through practical exercises and reflection prompts, individuals are encouraged to create a roadmap of goals tailored to their unique journey. The chapter underscores that progress, no matter how small, is a testament to resilience and a stepping stone toward a life less encumbered by anxiety.

Embracing Uncertainty and Imperfection

Anxiety often thrives in the realm of uncertainty, yet the journey to conquer it requires a willingness to embrace the unknown. This section explores strategies for navigating uncertainty, including mindfulness, cognitive reframing, and self-compassion. Readers discover how cultivating a mindset that acknowledges imperfection and uncertainty can lead to greater resilience and peace of mind.

The chapter encourages individuals to reframe their relationship with uncertainty, viewing it not as a source of fear but as an inherent and manageable aspect of life. By relinquishing the quest for absolute certainty, individuals pave the way for a more liberated and fulfilling existence.

Celebrating Achievements, No Matter How Small

In the pursuit of conquering anxiety, celebrating achievements, no matter how modest, becomes a crucial practice. This section delves into the significance of acknowledging progress, fostering self-compassion, and building a positive narrative. Readers learn to cultivate a mindset that values the journey and celebrates the resilience displayed in moments of growth.
Through reflection exercises and gratitude practices, individuals are encouraged to recognize their achievements and strengths. The chapter serves as a reminder that the path to overcoming anxiety is paved with small victories, each contributing to a life rich in fulfillment and self-discovery.

The Empowering Role of Support Systems

Facing fears and overcoming avoidance behaviors are often more manageable with the support of a nurturing network. This section explores how friends, family, and mental health professionals can play a pivotal role in providing encouragement, accountability, and perspective. Real-life stories highlight the transformative impact of supportive relationships on the journey to liberation.
By fostering open communication and enlisting the support of others, individuals gain strength in numbers as they confront fears and break free from avoidance patterns. The chapter emphasizes that seeking support is not a sign of weakness but a courageous step toward liberation.

Maintaining a Positive Outlook

In conclusion, this chapter underscores the importance of maintaining a positive outlook as a beacon guiding individuals through the challenges of overcoming fear and avoidance. The journey to liberation is a continual process of self-discovery and growth. As we explore the strategies within this chapter, remember that each step forward, no matter how small, contributes to the mosaic of a life liberated from the constraints of anxiety. The subsequent chapters will continue to build upon these foundations, exploring additional strategies and perspectives to further empower individuals on their quest for mental well-being.

Recognizing the Importance of Support

Supportive relationships become the bedrock of resilience in this section, as readers delve into the recognition of the importance of connection in their journey toward well-being. Real-life stories illustrate the pivotal role that supportive relationships play in navigating challenges, reducing anxiety, and fostering a sense of belonging.
The chapter invites individuals to reflect on their current support systems, acknowledging existing sources of strength and considering opportunities for cultivating additional connections. By recognizing the importance of support, individuals set the stage for a resilient foundation that enhances their ability to conquer anxiety.

Cultivating Connection

Building strong support systems is an intentional process that involves cultivating meaningful connections. This section unfolds as a guide to cultivating connection—whether through friendships, family bonds, or community involvement. Readers gain insights into the transformative potential of authentic relationships in fostering resilience and well-being. Practical tips for initiating and nurturing connections are provided, empowering individuals to build a network of relationships that supports their mental health journey. By fostering authentic connections, individuals not only conquer anxiety in times of need but also create a sense of community that uplifts and sustains them.

Effective Communication in Relationships

Effective communication becomes a cornerstone of supportive relationships in this section. The chapter explores the art of communicating openly, empathetically, and assertively in order to strengthen connections. Real-life examples illustrate how effective communication fosters understanding, reduces misunderstandings, and deepens emotional bonds.
Practical exercises guide individuals in honing their communication skills, fostering a sense of vulnerability and authenticity in relationships. By developing effective communication strategies, individuals create an environment that nurtures resilience and enhances their ability to navigate challenges together.

Setting Healthy Boundaries

Boundaries are essential in maintaining healthy and supportive relationships. This section unfolds as a guide to setting and respecting boundaries—a practice that empowers individuals to protect their well-being while fostering connection. Readers gain insights into the importance of clear communication, self-awareness, and mutual respect in boundary-setting.
The chapter provides practical tips for establishing and maintaining boundaries in various relationships, empowering individuals to create a supportive environment that aligns with their needs. By setting healthy boundaries, individuals not only protect their mental well-being but also contribute to the overall resilience of their support systems.

Seeking Professional Support

In some instances, seeking professional support becomes a vital aspect of building a comprehensive support system. This section explores the transformative role of therapy, counseling, and other mental health services in enhancing resilience. Real-life stories illuminate the impact of professional support on individuals' ability to conquer anxiety and cultivate lasting well-being.
Readers gain insights into the diverse therapeutic modalities available and the importance of finding a supportive and trustworthy mental health professional. The chapter encourages individuals to view seeking professional support as a proactive step toward strengthening their resilience and fostering mental flourishing.

Reciprocity and Supportive Relationships

The essence of reciprocity unfolds as a guiding principle in this section, emphasizing the mutual exchange of support within relationships. The chapter explores how giving and receiving support create a reciprocal flow of energy that fortifies the pillars of resilience. Real-life examples illustrate the transformative power of reciprocal support in fostering a sense of community and connection.

Practical exercises guide individuals in reflecting on ways to contribute to the well-being of others within their support systems. By embracing reciprocity, individuals not only conquer anxiety within the embrace of their support networks but also cultivate a culture of shared strength and resilience.

Fostering Resilience in Families

In conclusion, Chapter 9 unveils the profound impact of building strong support systems—the pillars of resilience that sustain individuals on their journey of conquering anxiety. It is an exploration into the transformative power of connection, effective communication, healthy boundaries, professional support, reciprocity, and the resilience fostered within families.

The subsequent chapters will continue to unveil additional dimensions of resilience, offering insights and practices to further empower individuals on their quest to conquer anxiety. By cultivating strong support systems, individuals not only illuminate the shadows of anxiety but also forge a path toward lasting well-being, surrounded by the strength and understanding of a supportive community.

Chapter 10. Maintaining Long-Term Mental Health: Strategies for Resilience

As we stand on the precipice of lasting transformation, this chapter navigates the terrain of maintaining long-term mental health. It is a culmination of insights, strategies, and perspectives gathered throughout the journey, offering a roadmap for resilience and sustained well-being.

Strategies for Relapse Prevention

The path to long-term mental health is not without challenges, and relapses may occur. This section explores strategies for relapse prevention, equipping individuals with tools to identify warning signs and navigate setbacks effectively. From developing coping mechanisms to recognizing triggers, readers gain insights into creating a proactive plan to safeguard their mental well-being.

Practical exercises and self-assessment tools are provided to empower individuals in building resilience against the ebb and flow of mental health challenges. By acknowledging that setbacks are a natural part of the journey, this chapter encourages a compassionate and forward-focused mindset.

Building a Lifestyle of Self-Care

Self-care is not a luxury but a foundational practice for maintaining long-term mental health. This section delves into the importance of cultivating a lifestyle that prioritizes self-care. Readers explore diverse self-care strategies, from creative pursuits and hobbies to mindfulness practices and healthy boundaries.

The chapter emphasizes that self-care is a dynamic and evolving practice, requiring individuals to continually reassess and adapt their routines to meet changing needs. By infusing self-care into daily life, individuals build a reservoir of strength to draw from during challenging times.

Nurturing Relationships and Connection

The strength of social connections continues to be a cornerstone of long-term mental health. This section revisits the role of relationships, highlighting the impact of nurturing connections on resilience. From fostering open communication to practicing empathy and understanding, readers gain insights into building and sustaining healthy relationships.

The chapter explores the reciprocity of support within relationships, emphasizing the importance of both giving and receiving. By maintaining a network of understanding individuals, individuals create a supportive ecosystem that bolsters their mental well-being.

Continuing the Journey of Self-Discovery

Long-term mental health is a journey of continual self-discovery and growth. This section encourages individuals to remain curious about themselves, their values, and their evolving aspirations. Through ongoing reflection, goal-setting, and exploration, readers learn to adapt and thrive in the ever-changing landscape of their lives.

The chapter also explores the concept of lifelong learning and the role of curiosity in mental well-being. By approaching life with an open heart and mind, individuals embrace the journey of self-discovery as a perpetual source of resilience.

Embracing a Life Beyond Anxiety

In conclusion, this chapter is an invitation to embrace a life beyond the shadows of anxiety. It underscores that the journey to long-term mental health is a dynamic and evolving process, requiring ongoing commitment and self-compassion. As we explore the strategies within this chapter, let us celebrate the resilience, growth, and liberation that each individual has achieved. The subsequent chapters will continue to offer guidance and insights, reinforcing the foundations of resilience and empowerment. By embracing the principles of relapse prevention, self-care, nurturing relationships, and ongoing self-discovery, individuals lay a robust groundwork for a life characterized by enduring mental well-being and fulfillment.

The Essence of Self-Compassion

Self-compassion emerges as a gentle companion in this section, inviting individuals to extend kindness, understanding, and warmth toward themselves. The chapter explores the core components of self-compassion—self-kindness, common humanity, and mindfulness—and their profound impact on mental well-being.

Real-life stories illuminate the transformative power of self-compassion in reducing anxiety, fostering emotional resilience, and cultivating a positive relationship with oneself. Practical exercises guide individuals in cultivating self-compassion, empowering them to navigate the complexities of life with grace and self-kindness.

Embracing Mindful Self-Care Practices

Mindful self-care becomes a cornerstone of resilience in this section, inviting individuals to engage in intentional and nurturing practices that foster well-being. Readers explore a diverse array of mindful self-care practices, from meditation and deep breathing to creative expression and nature connection.

The chapter provides practical tips for incorporating mindful self-care into daily life, emphasizing the importance of creating a personalized self-care routine. By embracing mindful self-care practices, individuals not only conquer anxiety in the moment but also cultivate a sustainable foundation for lasting well-being.

Setting Boundaries for Self-Care

Boundaries play a vital role in mindful self-care, enabling individuals to protect their well-being and prioritize activities that nourish the mind, body, and soul. This section unfolds as a guide to setting and respecting boundaries for self-care, emphasizing the importance of clear communication and self-awareness.

Real-life examples illustrate how healthy boundaries contribute to the effectiveness of self-care practices. The chapter provides practical exercises to help individuals identify and implement boundaries that support their well-being. By setting boundaries for self-care, individuals create a sanctuary of rejuvenation and resilience.

Nourishing the Mind, Body, and Soul

Mindful self-care extends beyond routine practices to encompass the holistic nourishment of the mind, body, and soul. This section explores the interconnectedness of these dimensions and offers insights into practices that promote overall well-being. Readers discover the transformative potential of activities such as nourishing nutrition, restorative sleep, and joyful movement.

The chapter encourages individuals to explore and integrate diverse practices that resonate with their unique needs and preferences. By nourishing the mind, body, and soul, individuals create a harmonious symphony of well-being that supports their journey of conquering anxiety.

Cultivating Joy and Gratitude

Joy and gratitude become guiding lights in the landscape of mindful self-care. This section invites individuals to explore practices that cultivate joy and gratitude, fostering a positive and resilient mindset. Real-life stories illustrate the transformative impact of incorporating joy and gratitude into daily life.

Practical exercises guide individuals in discovering sources of joy and practicing gratitude as intentional aspects of their self-care routine. By infusing joy and gratitude into their lives, individuals not only conquer anxiety but also create a tapestry of positivity and resilience that enriches their well-being.

Reflecting on Personal Growth

Mindful self-care becomes a journey of personal growth and self-discovery in this section. The chapter encourages individuals to reflect on their experiences, insights, and the ways in which mindful self-care has contributed to their growth. Readers gain insights into the transformative potential of self-reflection in fostering resilience and well-being.

Practical exercises guide individuals in creating a personal growth journal and setting intentions for continued self-care. By embracing reflective practices, individuals not only conquer anxiety in the moment but also embark on a journey of continuous personal evolution and thriving.

Building a Sustainable Self-Care Routine

In conclusion, Chapter 10 unfolds as an exploration into the transformative practices of self-compassion and mindful self-care—a holistic approach that empowers individuals to conquer anxiety and thrive in the rich tapestry of life. It is an invitation to cultivate self-kindness, set boundaries, nourish the mind, body, and soul, and infuse joy and gratitude into daily life. As we conclude this chapter, let the essence of self-compassion and mindful self-care resonate in your heart. The subsequent chapters will serve as a synthesis of the journey, offering a roadmap for continued growth, resilience, and enduring well-being. By embracing self-compassion and mindful self-care, individuals not only conquer anxiety but also create a life characterized by inner strength, joy, and a profound connection to the wellspring of their own resilience.

Chapter 11. Cultivating Mindful Living: A Blueprint for Lasting Well-Being

As we approach the pinnacle of our journey towards lasting well-being, this chapter explores the transformative philosophy of mindful living. It serves as a blueprint, guiding individuals to integrate mindfulness into every facet of their lives, fostering enduring mental health and a profound sense of fulfillment.

The Essence of Mindful Living

Mindful living is not a mere practice; it is a way of being. This section delves into the essence of mindful living, emphasizing the cultivation of present-moment awareness in all aspects of daily life. From routine activities to significant life events, readers gain insights into infusing intention and attention into every experience.

Through practical examples and guided exercises, individuals learn to apply mindfulness to diverse areas, including relationships, work, and personal pursuits. By embracing mindful living, individuals embark on a journey of profound self-discovery and connection with the world around them.

Mindful Communication and Relationships

Healthy and fulfilling relationships thrive on the bedrock of mindful communication. This section explores the principles of mindful communication, highlighting the importance of active listening, empathy, and non-judgmental presence. Readers gain practical tools to foster deeper connections with others, transforming their relationships into sources of support and understanding.

The chapter also addresses the concept of mindful conflict resolution, offering strategies for navigating disagreements with compassion and clarity. By integrating mindfulness into interpersonal dynamics, individuals create a harmonious environment that nurtures their mental well-being.

Mindful Work and Productivity

The demands of the modern workplace often contribute to stress and anxiety. This section introduces mindfulness as a powerful tool for navigating work-related challenges. From managing stress to enhancing creativity and focus, readers discover how mindfulness practices can elevate their professional lives.

Practical tips for incorporating mindfulness into daily work routines are provided, empowering individuals to cultivate a mindful approach to productivity. By fostering a balanced and centered mindset, individuals navigate the professional landscape with resilience and purpose.

Mindful Eating and Physical Well-Being

Nutrition transcends mere sustenance when approached with mindfulness. This section explores the concept of mindful eating, encouraging individuals to savor the sensory experience of each meal. From recognizing hunger and fullness cues to cultivating gratitude for nourishing foods, readers learn to build a positive and balanced relationship with food.

The chapter also explores the intersection of mindfulness and physical activity, emphasizing the joy of movement and the integration of mindfulness practices into exercise routines. By approaching physical well-being with mindfulness, individuals foster a holistic and sustainable approach to health.

Mindfulness in Daily Rituals and Habits

The fabric of mindful living is woven into the daily rituals and habits that shape our lives. This section provides insights into infusing mindfulness into morning routines, bedtime rituals, and other daily habits. By approaching each moment with intention and awareness, individuals create a tapestry of mindful living that supports their overall well-being.

Practical exercises and reflection prompts guide readers in identifying opportunities for mindfulness in their daily lives. The chapter underscores that mindfulness is not a separate practice but a thread woven seamlessly into the fabric of existence.

The Journey Beyond Anxiety

In conclusion, this chapter is an invitation to embark on the journey beyond anxiety through the transformative practice of mindful living. It underscores that mindfulness is not a destination but a continuous exploration of the present moment. As we integrate mindfulness into communication, relationships, work, nutrition, and daily rituals, we cultivate a life characterized by enduring well-being, purpose, and joy.

The subsequent chapters will continue to provide guidance and insights, reinforcing the foundations of mindful living and its role in maintaining mental health. By embracing the principles of mindfulness, individuals not only break free from the shadows of anxiety but also step into a life illuminated by the beauty and richness of each passing moment.

Reflecting on the Journey

This section invites individuals to pause and reflect on their personal journey, acknowledging the challenges faced, victories celebrated, and the transformative moments that have shaped their path. Readers are encouraged to explore the evolution of their understanding of anxiety and the insights gained along the way.

The chapter provides reflective exercises, encouraging individuals to journal their reflections and insights. By looking back on the journey, individuals gain a deeper understanding of their resilience, growth, and the inner resources that have empowered them to conquer anxiety.

Crafting a Personal Well-Being Plan

Building on the insights gathered throughout the journey, this section guides individuals in crafting a personalized well-being plan—a roadmap for continued growth, resilience, and enduring joy. Readers explore the integration of mindfulness practices, self-compassion, intentional growth mindset, and other transformative tools into their daily lives.

Practical exercises empower individuals to set specific goals, identify supportive practices, and establish a framework for lifelong well-being. By creating a personal well-being plan, individuals not only solidify their commitment to lasting well-being but also cultivate a roadmap that aligns with their unique values and aspirations.

Navigating Setbacks with Resilience

Setbacks are a natural part of any journey, and this section unfolds as a guide to navigating setbacks with resilience and self-compassion. Readers explore how the insights gained from the journey can be applied to overcome challenges, bounce back from setbacks, and continue on the path of well-being.

The chapter provides practical strategies for reframing setbacks, seeking support, and embracing self-compassion during challenging times. By navigating setbacks with resilience, individuals reinforce their ability to conquer anxiety and move forward with a sense of strength and purpose.

Cultivating a Growth Mindset

The journey of conquering anxiety is a continual process of growth and self-discovery. This section emphasizes the importance of cultivating a growth mindset—a belief in the potential for ongoing development and learning. Readers explore how adopting a growth mindset contributes to resilience, adaptability, and a positive outlook on life.

Practical exercises guide individuals in fostering a growth mindset, challenging limiting beliefs, and embracing opportunities for learning. By cultivating a growth mindset, individuals not only conquer anxiety but also approach life's challenges with curiosity, optimism, and a sense of continual development.

Sustaining Resilience Through Community

Community becomes a sustaining force in the pursuit of well-being. This section explores the importance of maintaining connections with supportive communities—whether through friends, family, or like-minded individuals. Real-life stories highlight the transformative power of communal support in fostering resilience, reducing isolation, and sustaining well-being.

The chapter provides practical tips for nurturing and expanding supportive connections, fostering a sense of belonging and reciprocity. By sustaining resilience through community, individuals create a network of strength and understanding that fortifies their journey toward lasting well-being.

40

Embracing a Lifestyle of Well-Being

The integration of well-being practices into daily life becomes a focal point in this section.
Readers are encouraged to embrace a lifestyle of well-being by consistently incorporating
mindful practices, self-care rituals, and intentional growth strategies into their routines.
Practical exercises guide individuals in identifying opportunities for well-being in various aspects
of their lives, from relationships to work and leisure. By embracing a lifestyle of well-being,
individuals not only conquer anxiety but also create a sustainable and fulfilling way of living that
aligns with their values and aspirations.

Celebrating Milestones and Growth

As individuals progress on their journey, it is essential to celebrate milestones and acknowledge
personal growth. This section invites readers to reflect on the achievements and transformations
that have occurred, fostering a sense of accomplishment and appreciation for the resilience
demonstrated.
The chapter provides reflective exercises for individuals to celebrate their milestones, reinforcing
the positive aspects of their journey. By celebrating milestones and growth, individuals cultivate
a mindset of gratitude and self-appreciation that contributes to enduring well-being.

Embodying a Life Well-Lived

In conclusion, Chapter 11 unfolds as a synthesis and integration of the journey—a celebration of
conquering anxiety and embodying a life well-lived. It is an invitation for individuals to carry
forward the wisdom gained, the transformative practices embraced, and the resilience cultivated
into every aspect of their lives.
The subsequent sections will serve as a testament to the enduring well-being that individuals
can continue to foster. By reflecting on the journey, crafting a personal well-being plan,
navigating setbacks with resilience, cultivating a growth mindset, sustaining resilience through
community, embracing a lifestyle of well-being, and celebrating milestones and growth,
individuals not only conquer anxiety but also embark on a lifelong journey of resilience, joy, and
enduring well-being.

Chapter 12. Embracing Resilience: A Lifelong Journey of Growth

In the final chapter of our transformative journey, we explore the profound concept of resilience—a quality that not only defines our ability to overcome challenges but shapes our ongoing journey of personal growth and fulfillment. This chapter serves as a compass, guiding individuals towards a life characterized by strength, adaptability, and a continual pursuit of self-discovery.

The Essence of Resilience

Resilience is not a fixed trait but a dynamic quality that can be cultivated and strengthened over time. This section delves into the essence of resilience, emphasizing its role in bouncing back from adversity and navigating life's inevitable ups and downs. Through real-life stories and examples, readers gain insights into the diverse ways individuals have embraced resilience to triumph over challenges.

The chapter introduces the concept of a growth mindset—the belief that challenges and setbacks are opportunities for learning and development. By fostering a growth mindset, individuals approach life with a sense of optimism and a willingness to embrace the journey of continuous improvement.

Cultivating Resilience Through Adversity

Adversity is an inevitable part of the human experience, and resilience becomes a guiding light in times of hardship. This section explores strategies for cultivating resilience during challenging moments. From reframing adversity as an opportunity for growth to developing problem-solving skills and seeking support, readers gain practical tools to navigate difficult circumstances with resilience and grace.

The chapter also highlights the importance of self-compassion during challenging times. By treating oneself with kindness and understanding, individuals foster a resilient mindset that propels them forward on the path to lasting well-being.

Navigating Transitions and Change

Life is a series of transitions, each presenting its unique set of challenges and opportunities. This section explores the role of resilience in navigating life transitions, whether they be career changes, relationship shifts, or personal transformations. Readers gain insights into adapting to change with flexibility and embracing the uncertainty that comes with new beginnings.

Practical exercises and reflection prompts guide individuals in developing a resilience toolkit tailored to their unique journey. By approaching transitions with a resilient mindset, individuals not only weather the storms of change but also harness the potential for personal growth and self-discovery.

Resilience in Relationships

Resilience is not only an individual trait but also a quality that can enhance the fabric of relationships. This section explores how resilient communication, conflict resolution, and empathy contribute to the strength of interpersonal connections. Readers gain insights into fostering resilient relationships that provide support and encouragement during life's challenges. The chapter emphasizes the reciprocity of resilience within relationships, highlighting the transformative power of shared experiences and mutual growth. By building resilient connections, individuals create a network of support that fortifies their mental well-being.

Resilience as a Lifelong Practice

In conclusion, this chapter underscores that resilience is not a destination but a lifelong practice. It is a commitment to embracing challenges, learning from setbacks, and continually adapting to the evolving landscape of life. As we navigate the principles of resilience, let us recognize that every moment, whether joyful or challenging, contributes to the tapestry of our unique and ever-unfolding journey.

The subsequent chapters have laid the foundation for enduring well-being, providing guidance on conquering anxiety, fostering mindfulness, and embracing a life characterized by growth and fulfillment. By integrating the principles of resilience into our lives, we not only break free from the shadows of anxiety but also embark on a lifelong journey of resilience, strength, and the continual pursuit of a meaningful and flourishing existence.

Embracing the Spirit of Curiosity

The journey toward a lifetime of well-being is marked by a spirit of curiosity—an openness to exploring new possibilities, cultivating a sense of wonder, and embracing the ongoing adventure of self-discovery. This section encourages individuals to nurture their curiosity as a guiding force that propels them forward on the path of well-being.

Readers explore the transformative power of curiosity in fostering creativity, adaptability, and a vibrant approach to life. Practical exercises guide individuals in incorporating curiosity into their daily routines, fostering a lifelong mindset of exploration and discovery.

Deepening Connections with Self and Others

Connection remains at the heart of a life well-lived, and this section delves into the significance of deepening connections—with oneself, others, and the world. Real-life stories illuminate how profound connections contribute to a sense of purpose, joy, and sustained well-being.

The chapter provides practical tips for deepening connections, from engaging in meaningful conversations to fostering a sense of presence in relationships. By prioritizing and nurturing connections, individuals create a rich tapestry of relationships that support their journey toward a lifetime of well-being.

Living in Alignment with Values

A life well-lived is one that is aligned with one's core values. This section explores the importance of clarifying and living in alignment with personal values—a compass that guides choices, actions, and the overall trajectory of life.

Readers engage in reflective exercises to identify and prioritize their values, ensuring that daily decisions align with their authentic selves. By living in alignment with values, individuals not only conquer anxiety but also cultivate a sense of purpose and fulfillment that sustains them throughout their lives.

Embracing Lifelong Learning

Lifelong learning continues to be a cornerstone of a thriving life, and this section encourages individuals to embrace a spirit of continual education and growth. The chapter explores the diverse avenues for learning, from formal education to self-directed exploration, and highlights the transformative impact of intellectual and creative stimulation.

Practical exercises guide individuals in identifying areas of interest and setting goals for ongoing learning. By embracing lifelong learning, individuals not only conquer anxiety but also cultivate a curious and agile mind that contributes to their overall well-being.

Savoring Moments of Joy

Savoring the richness of life becomes a daily practice in this section, inviting individuals to cultivate mindfulness and gratitude for the small, joyful moments that contribute to a life well-lived. Real-life stories illustrate how savoring enhances the experience of joy and fosters a positive outlook on life.

The chapter provides practical exercises for individuals to incorporate savoring practices into their daily routines, enhancing their ability to appreciate and derive meaning from everyday moments. By savoring moments of joy, individuals create a reservoir of positivity that contributes to their overall well-being.

Fostering a Legacy of Well-Being

As individuals embark on a lifetime of well-being, they have the opportunity to shape a legacy of resilience, connection, and positive impact. This section encourages individuals to reflect on the contributions they want to make to their communities, families, and the world.

Readers engage in exercises to identify their values, passions, and the ways in which they can contribute to the well-being of others. By fostering a legacy of well-being, individuals not only conquer anxiety but also leave a positive imprint on the world, creating a lasting impact for generations to come.

Embracing the Journey

In conclusion, Chapter 12 unfolds as an embrace of the lifelong journey toward well-being—an ongoing exploration of curiosity, deepening connections, living in alignment with values, embracing lifelong learning, savoring moments of joy, and fostering a legacy of well-being. It is an invitation for individuals to continue navigating the path with resilience, purpose, and a profound connection to the richness of life.

As we conclude this exploration, may the wisdom gained serve as a guiding light for a lifetime of well-being. The subsequent sections will offer closing reflections, resources, and encouragement for individuals to carry forward the insights and practices into every chapter of their lives. By embracing the spirit of curiosity, deepening connections, living in alignment with values, embracing lifelong learning, savoring moments of joy, and fostering a legacy of well-being, individuals not only conquer anxiety but also embark on a lifelong journey of resilience, joy, and enduring well-being.

Final Message: A Journey of Liberation and Growth

Dear Reader,

As we conclude this transformative journey together, I want to extend my heartfelt congratulations on your commitment to self-discovery, resilience, and lasting well-being. The path you've walked has been one of courage, exploration, and profound growth.

From unraveling the complexities of anxiety to embracing the philosophy of mindful living and resilience, you've shown an unwavering dedication to your own flourishing. The insights gained, the strategies learned, and the moments of self-reflection have all played a part in shaping a life that transcends the constraints of anxiety.

Remember that this journey is not a linear one. It's a continual exploration, a dance with the ever-changing rhythms of life. As you move forward, know that you carry within you the tools of resilience, the wisdom of mindfulness, and the strength forged in the crucible of your own experiences.

Life is a canvas, and each day is an opportunity to paint it with the vibrant colors of your choices, your growth, and your self-discovery. Celebrate the victories, both big and small. Embrace the challenges as invitations to learn and evolve. In the tapestry of your existence, may you find beauty in the journey itself.

As you step into the chapters yet to be written, may you navigate with grace, courage, and an enduring commitment to your well-being. Your story is one of liberation, growth, and the ongoing pursuit of a life rich in meaning and fulfillment.

Wishing you boundless joy, resilience, and the profound satisfaction that comes from living a life true to yourself.

With warmth and encouragement,

Gregory Hart